18 Holes in Leadership

Thomas J. McSweeney Jr.

DEDICATION

This book is dedicated to my coach, Ernie Hughes, whose constant encouragement prompted me to use my abilities to pursue my passions.

And to my best friend/wife/editor, Kristi, whose passion encouraged me to use those abilities.

CONTENTS

INTRODUCTION

This past summer I was having the Northwest's interpretation of a Philly Cheesesteak with my executive coach at a tiny restaurant in Issaquah, WA. I had met Ernie Hughes two years prior in the summer of 2015 after a class he delivered on "Managing Agile". He had used the Rocky movies during his lecture in a kind of disparaging way which didn't quite seem to fit with his point. I contacted him afterwards and asked if he'd ever seen the other films. Ernie admitted that he hadn't but that he would accept the challenge and add them to his movie queue.

He wrote me an email a while later, having viewed *all* of the Rocky movies (though he probably could have skipped over <u>Rocky IV</u>) and, to his pleasant surprise, admitted that they were quite inspirational. He invited me to lunch for the aforementioned "cheesesteaks" and we have been friends ever since.

Ernie is super smart and we'll meet periodically to discuss some professional impediment or quandary that I'm facing. My topic during this particular meal revolved around work/life balance: does it really exist and, if so, how do I get it? Of course, Ernie never answers my questions directly and instead, launched into his Socratic method.

"Why do you ask?" he began.

"As I'm beginning my search for what I want to be when I grow up, I want to be sure that I'm considering work/life balance...assuming it exists."

"Oh, it certainly exists. But what does it look like to you?"

Gosh, does this guy ever answer a question? I figured I'd turn the tables and ask him a question. "You're asking me to describe the thing when I'm questioning its very existence?"

"Okay, let me ask it this way: If you had work/life balance, how would you know you had it?"

Didn't I tell you this guy was good! "Well, I've never lived to the exclusion of my work but I have done the reverse on a number of occasions. I suppose if I had balance, it wouldn't feel like I was so deprived."

Ernie furrowed his brow. "Perhaps this has less to do with balance and more to do with passion. What are you passionate about?"

"Professionally? Solving problems. I love taking complex situations, making them simple, and then resolving them through a team effort."

"Okay," he began, nodding. "And what are you passionate about in your personal life?"

"You mean besides my wife?"

He laughed. "Yes. Besides Kristi."

"Golf," I replied immediately.

"Write about that!"

"Write about solving business problems and golf? They're not related." I was beginning to think I may have overestimated Ernie's greatness.

"Maybe not at the moment they're not but they will be when you're finished." He smiled, stood, and left the restaurant. Evidently, our session was over.

I went home and thought about this crazy assignment. Was it really possible to link the two? I turned on the computer and stared at the blank Word document for about an hour, waiting for inspiration. The cursor continuously blinked at me; the page remained blank. I ended my quest for work/life balance and sought solace through some kitten videos on YouTube.

About three months later, I was giving a lecture to a group of customer service professionals about breaking down the virtual, corporate walls that divide us. A woman in the audience asked a question about my scorecard (I won't spoil the whole story here. You can read about it in Chapter 1.) She had made an excellent point and I was trying to think of an analogy to explain my reasoning. Yup, you guessed it! A golf analogy leapt into my head! In fact, it was such a befitting explanation that I was a bit surprised that I had never considered it before that moment.

On the drive home, I was still mulling it over when I realized what I had done. I had completed Ernie's challenge by combining my two passions. I wrote it down and had my wife proofread it for me. When I finished the corrections, I sent it to Ernie.

He wrote back, "Congrats, Tom. 17 more."

Seventeen more? It took me three months to come up with the first one! Was he crazy? This was shaping up to be a four and a half year undertaking.

But I accepted the assignment with the same grace that he had accepted the Rocky challenge. For the next four months, I would document another lesson learned and send it to Ernie for his review. He would always send back some encouraging words and then let me know how many more stories I needed to finish.

Then one day, it was complete. I sent the eighteenth essay to Ernie and he wrote back, "Congratulations, Tom, on finishing the draft of your next book." That sneaky genius! He had tricked me into writing a collection of short stories and in the process, I learned what work/life balance was.

As long as I saw work and life as competitors for the same resource, namely time, I was always going to be out of balance. However, by merging them together, I discovered that one could flow into the other. Things that I learned in my daily life could prepare me to be successful at work.

For instance, let's say that you deposit your paycheck, pay your bills, and balance your checkbook. Surely some of that experience could translate into your career in finance. Or let's say that you were foolish enough to accept a position on your HOA board and had to deal with all the petty complaints that residents were constantly dumping on you. Could any of those experiences better prepare you for your career in customer service? And if you have ever raised toddlers, you know exactly what its like to manage a group of software engineers. If we can combine what we do for a living with what we enjoy in our free time, we have a pretty good chance of creating balance.

As I mentioned before, one of my passions, along with finding solutions to business problems, is the game of golf. While I admit to having far more success with the former, I have also found a great deal of lessons that arise from the latter. As a result, I have written this series of essays that I hope you will find both entertaining and profitable. I tried to keep the book succinct enough so that it could be read in about the same amount of time as a round of golf.

If any of them resonate with you, please reach out to me on LinkedIn[i] and let me know. Or better yet, if you're dealing with a leadership problem and one of them leads to an "aha moment", please leave me a comment on Amazon!

HOLE #1: A DRIVE AND A PUTT

I was recently giving a talk to a professional group of customer service and support professionals in Bellevue.   Afterwards, one of the attendees approached me with a question:

"You mentioned in one of your solutions to Breaking Down Our Virtual Walls that we create and publicize our scorecards." [The scorecard is derived from a collection of common, cross-functional goals.] "Your example cited a depreciation for each outage but we know that all outages are not created equal. Some involve a loss of service to millions while others only negatively affect a few hundred. Surely you're not suggesting that we measure them the same, are you?"

Great question and one that I've struggled with many times before! It stems from a callousness that starts to develop over time in our service industries.

It's not that we don't care about our customers – of course we do! – they are our lifeblood and reason for being. But after a while, they become numbers rather than people: "We had an outage last night during the maintenance window that affected 150 customers. At least it wasn't as bad as that outage we had last year!" It's natural to put things into perspective and 150-customer outage is certainly less painful than impacting 150,000…unless you are one of those 150 without service.

And that's where the inequity of golf has taught me a valuable lesson. For many years I have struggled with the fact that my 250-yard drive and my 3-foot putt each count as one stroke. It doesn't seem fair that hitting the ball 2 ½ football fields with one swing would count the same as hitting it half the length of my body! And it becomes particularly painful when my 3-foot putt stops right at the lip of the cup! My seemingly certain par has just become a bogey instead!

So I answered her question by relating my golf analogy and espousing the following two benefits to measuring outages with the same weight:

Firstly, it makes it easier to measure. One of the things you need to consider when developing your company's scorecard is your ability to maintain it. Imagine what my golf scorecard would look like if that putt were weighted against my drive. Three feet would count as $1/4,400$ of a stroke. But it stopped right on the lip so I'd have to subtract $1/500,000$ of a stroke from that shot. And we haven't even calculated my approach shot or chip onto the green yet! The simpler you can keep your math, the better.

But more importantly, counting outages the same shows a commitment to our customers. Whether our actions (or inactions) have negatively affected one or a million and one subscribers of our service, they are each a person who was counting on you to do your job.

If our goal is "near-zero defects", why should it matter how many people were impacted? Take your lumps, record your bogey, and vow to do better next time. And whatever you do, never leave a putt short! There's no chance of it falling into the cup for a par!

HOLE #2: FOREST THROUGH THE TREES

I wouldn't have difficulty scoring if every fairway was 200 yards wide like it is on the driving range. I suppose that's why I always leave there feeling like I know what I'm doing only to be slapped back into reality out on the actual course. Where two or more trees are gathered, inevitably, there also will be my ball. I shouldn't go to the range to practice; I should just take a bunch of balls into the woods and practice hitting out.

And that's when it struck me – almost literally! After hitting my drive into a clump of trees on the edge of the 13th fairway, I could see a narrow sliver of daylight with the green about 160 yards beyond that. I knew during my back swing that this was an ill-advised shot! The chance of me threading the needle was about 100:1. But I took it anyway, the ball hit squarely into the 4th tree, and ricocheted straight back at my head! Had I not ducked at that moment, I would have had a tattoo on my forehead that read "tsieltiT" (Titleist spelled backwards).

What made me take that low probability shot? Even though it had trickled into the grove, my drive had traveled over 270 yards! (Admittedly, it probably would have stopped well short of that had the summer sun not scorched the fairway.) Despite the low probability of success, I now had a chance to hit the green in two and hole out for an eagle! I could almost hear the roar of the crowd as I addressed the ball.

The smart play would have been to hit laterally back into the fairway, then onto the green in regulation, and two putts for a par. Someone once said that the best thing you can do when you find yourself in a hole is to stop digging. Good advice and one that segues nicely from golf to business.

Why, when we find ourselves in a professional predicament, do we try to hit through that sliver of daylight? Taking an approach other than the one directly in front of you could mean a variety of things. For me it meant leaving my comfortable job in order to pursue what I really wanted to do. But we fool ourselves into driving forward through the obstacles rather than sideways around them because we think forward is progress, especially when the goal is peeking out through the canopy. I would convince myself that I could bend my current job into my passion, knowing full well that the likelihood was slim.

So today I was telling my golf buddy my idea for this essay when I yanked my second shot through the trees and onto the neighboring fairway. For a moment I thought, "I can still hit the green from here!" How ironic is it that I had just finished talking about the concept of shrewd course management and here I was considering an impossible shot?

When I wisely hit back into our fairway, rejoining my buddy, I confessed to the temptation of "going for it." As a successful business owner, he told me that sometimes the best way forward is backwards. For instance, he would forego some initial profits on a sale in order to establish a new customer and make more money in future volume. I could see the obvious insight to his approach, considering options in 360 degrees. I thanked him for his contribution and informed him I'd be stealing it to sum up my point: Seeing the forest through the trees means identifying your way forward, even if that path is behind you.

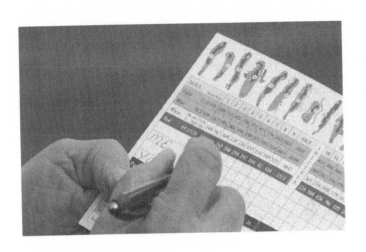

HOLE #3: THE COMPETITION

One of the things I love most about the game of golf is that I am the competition and not the people I'm playing with. Think about it. Every other game I can think of: tennis (and similar games like racquetball, badminton, pickle ball, etc.), bocce, pool, darts (of the English or lawn variety), and even shuffleboard, the object is to beat the other player. In golf, you can actually root for the other guy because his success has no bearing on yours. As a result, you can play golf with anyone of any caliber. Well, almost anyone.

A mutual friend recently introduced me to a fellow avid golfer over text message. I guess my friend was trying to set up a play date or something. The golfer and I chatted over text and agreed to play a course the following day. Then, as almost an aside, he asked me what my handicap was. Sarcastically I replied, "High enough to qualify for a parking space." That ended the conversation and I never heard back from the golfer again. Turns out he was a bit of a snob and would not play with anyone who shoots higher than 80.

But I don't mind playing with anyone. Well, anyone except for golf snobs. As a result, I am able to play with both scratch golfers and people who are just learning the game like my wife, so long as we're all enjoying ourselves.

Like all of the essays in this series, lessons in golf carry over to business. Our companies are made up of diverse levels of talents and, so long as we aren't competing with one another, we can have a lot of fun together. Whether we're challenging our personal best or striving toward a mutual goal, we're at our best when we're all going in the same direction. That's not to say that competition is bad. I am very competitive and truly believe that it brings about the best results. But I'm not competing against my team; I'm competing with them.

And just like golf, if your coworker is not your opponent, you can share information that will make him stronger. I have been struggling lately with chipping and end up skulling the ball to the other side of the green more often than not. My golfing buddy showed me a trick that now gets me within a makeable putt. He didn't lose anything by teaching me his method and I only gained from it. Same thing holds true in the office. People say that knowledge is power and they are correct. But it only becomes powerful when it is shared. And that's a great way to measure success on the course or in the office: When people ask you how you do something and start copying what you tell them.

HOLE #4: SQUIRREL!

I went golfing yesterday and witnessed a particularly troubling, uncontrollable habit begin to develop: I could not keep my head down. As any avid golfer will tell you, ninety percent of our errant shots are due to picking up our head during our swing. It causes the club to lift up ever so slightly and hit the top of the ball rather than the sweet spot.

I would visualize my shot, take a practice swing (which I could tell was perfect as it barely clipped the fairway grass), and then swing with my head popping up and the ball nose-diving into the ground. As I analyzed the situation, I came to the realization that I was trying to watch the flight of my ball before actually hitting it. Despite repeated attempts at convincing myself to keep my head down, I inexorably popped it up at the last moment.

And then the business parallel hit me: How often do we fail to execute because we take our proverbial eye off the ball?

- We "visualize our shot" by creating a mental image of where we want our business to go.
- We take a "practice swing" by mapping out a plan of how we're going to get there.
- And then we "pop our head up" by getting distracted with the results before we even execute the plan.

If you've ever seen the Pixar movie <u>Up</u>, there's a running joke where the dogs get distracted each time one of them says, "Squirrel!" They stop mid-sentence and pick their heads up, directing their gaze toward the rodent in question. In the same way, this momentary lapse of focus can cause our ball or our project to veer off course (pun intended). So for heaven's sake, keep your head down and your eye on the ball.

HOLE #5: ONE BITE AT A TIME

I had been playing golf for twenty years before I took my first lesson. I improved considerably over those initial decades but my score had begun to plateau. There was a time when I would have sold my soul to play "bogey golf" and feel that I had gotten the better part of the bargain. But my never-ending thirst to reduce that 18 handicap led me to seek professional help.

The pro had me hit a bucket of balls as he watched. Then he filmed me hitting a second bucket and fed the video into his computer. After several minutes of analysis he announced, "Everything is perfect except for your grip, your stance, and your swing."

"That sounds terrible," I replied. "What's left?"

"Nothing, I'm afraid."

He showed me the video he shot and it looked perfectly fine to me. Then, he showed me Tiger Wood's video and superimposed my image on top of his. There were obvious differences! The pro proceeded to make adjustments to my "everything" and had me hit another bucket as he filmed. I felt about as off balanced as an elephant on a unicycle. He made more adjustments and still more.

The next day, he had me hit another bucket of balls as he reinforced all of the adjustments that I'd forgotten from the previous lesson. Then, with my new Tiger grip, stance, and swing, we went out on the course to play 18 holes. It may be hyperbole to claim that it was the worst game of my life but it most certainly was in the worst ten! We resumed our lesson the following day with much the same outcome.

Trying to simultaneously change that many aspects of my game was a bit too daunting and ambitious, not to mention unprofitable. And yet I have made the exact same mistake in business. For years I had made a career out of saving failing projects. Most of the time, it was simply a matter of completing that final 20% of the original scope where my predecessors had either lost interest or focus. Then I was introduced to a group that put the "fun" in "dysfunctional". Just like my golf game, every aspect needed correction, and I tackled them all at the same time. Needless to say, the results were disastrous.

I had forgotten the virtues of incremental improvements that I had routinely employed during my years of software development. Back then, I had successfully reshaped my waterfall methodology into a more agile, evolutionary prototyping technique. As my grandmother used to always admonish me with her folksy wisdom, "You've got to crawl before you can walk, Tommy." After failing to improve my new charges, I took a step back. I began triaging the situation, addressing the most critical opportunities first, and then taking baby steps to correct them. My new mantra became, "Let's just make tomorrow look better than yesterday."

My golf game still needs some work but I'm happy to report that dysfunctional group of individuals became the highest performing team I have ever had the privilege of leading. We ate that unicycle-riding elephant – one bite at a time!

HOLE #6: GRIP IT AND RIP IT!

Hole #6[ii] is a narrow, short (only 296 yards) par four. The right side is out of bounds; the left side is a steep hill covered by trees. Forty yards off either side approaching the green is a tree. The only safe place to hit the ball is center-right in the fairway. And yet, every time I get to hole #6, I hit one of those TaylorMade knock-off drivers with the little adjustable weights in the head, allegedly to correct the flight of the ball.

Now I know two things for certain as I walk up on the tee box with the "toaster on a stick" in my hand:

1. I only hit that club straight about 70% of the time.

2. I can't hit the ball 300 yards.

That means that no matter how well I hit it, I'm still going to have a second shot before I reach the green. And, there's a 30% chance that my tee shot is going out of bounds, off a cliff, or behind a tree. On the other hand, my 4 iron is much more reliable. I can hit it straight, 200 yards, with a nice little draw about 90% of the time (provided I don't pop my head up – Squirrel!). Why don't I hit 4 iron instead of driver, you may ask?

- Because the Lord hates a coward!
- "Just grip it and rip it!"
- Obviously the truth of the matter is, because I'm not using course management at that moment. Just like in corporate management, the apparent choice is not always the correct one.

I had a guy working for me that was absolutely brilliant. He forgot more than I'll ever know and he rarely forgot a thing! He not only knew the ins and outs of our platform, he was also well versed in the systems upstream and downstream from ours. And most surprisingly, unlike the rest of my engineers, his writing was eloquent. I didn't need a Rosetta Stone to be able to understand his Status Reports!

So what do you do with an intelligent, well-written, well-informed employee? You put him in charge of composing your knowledgebase, of course! We met several times to plan our attack because we were essentially starting with a blank slate. We collaboratively outlined the content and set deadlines for each section. While "Rain Man" (he loved that nickname, by the way) was busy composing articles, I busied myself with organizing the new HTML repository.

At the end of the first deadline, I asked to read what he had written so far. His editorial looked "remarkably like the outline" we had sketched out weeks earlier. Undeterred, I asked Rain Man how long it was going to take him to flesh out the content and we agreed to meet again at the end of the month. But the end of the month came before his documentation was complete.

I wondered what was impeding his progress and he told me something astounding! He doesn't like writing.

"But you're so good at it!" I argued.

"Sure, I can do it. But I hate doing it. It takes me hours just to write my weekly status report."

I was stunned. How could I have been so myopic? I had the right guy in the wrong job! Just because he could do it didn't mean he should. As we continued our conversation, I found that he liked teaching with PowerPoint more than writing full-blown documentation. And therein lies our solution. He would teach the team while I would take copious notes. Afterward, I would organize my notes into articles and post them to our knowledgebase (since I actually enjoy writing) for the team to refer back to post-training. No more "grip it and rip it". My job was to put each member of my team in a position where he could be most successful.

P.S. Does that mean that now I walk up on the 6th tee with a 4 iron in my hand? Hell no! Lord hates a coward! Fore!

HOLE #7: THE PIT OF DESPAIR

I played the Jack Nicklaus designed Snoqualmie Ridge Golf Course[iii] for the first time last weekend. Based on the number of sand traps, I would say that the Golden Bear was in a rather vindictive mood; there are fifteen on the 18th hole alone! And these are not the average traps that you'd find on most municipal courses. These bunkers are dug like fallout shelters, halfway to China, with overhanging lips towering 10 to 15 feet above your head. When my ball found more than its fair share of these obstacles, I would enter The Princess Bride's Pit of Despair[iv] with the rake, my sand wedge, and a false hope for par.

Digging my heels in by wiggling them back and

forth like I'd seen the pros do on television, I envisioned the ball flying onto the green with a flurry of sand in its wake. In reality, I watched the ball smack directly into the bunker's lip and slowly roll back to its point of origin at my entrenched feet! Then, in an effort to demonstrate the definition of insanity, I watched it happen again...and again! At this point it dawns on me that my best chance of egress is to turn around and aim at the point of ingress; but, I rationalize, I've already invested three strokes and I can't afford two more! So I dig my heels in a little more and try to pick the ball clean - only to watch it fly over the green and into another bunker waiting on the far side.

Have you ever trapped yourself in a job where you knew you didn't belong? In some cases, you've had quite a bit of success along the way only to land in the proverbial trap. You tell yourself that you've already invested so much that you can't afford to back out now. But you know that you're in a pit based on the despair you feel each morning when the alarm clock rings. So you dig in your heels and diligently report to your self-imposed torture chamber.

I've had experiences like that before, too. Sometimes the culture that initially attracted you to the position begins to morph over time; sometimes it was all smoke and mirrors and never actually existed at all. Whatever the situation, there are three aspects to any job and you only control two: "Desire, Opportunity, and Ability." (It is purely a coincidence that these aspects form the acronym "DOA", though that does make it easier to remember!) Your boss sets the parameters of the opportunity while you have to decide if you have the ability and desire to meet his expectations.

In my last position, I managed a newly formed group that was comprised of remnants of recently disbanded departments. In particular, there was a hardworking Oracle DBA on my team that my boss wanted managed out of the organization. While I was getting to know Fred (not his real name), I found that his passion was administering databases but his title was "Software Engineer". I saw that Fred certainly had the aptitude and ability to do the job; however, he was forcing himself to do something that he didn't enjoy and it showed in his performance. I started asking around to find if any other team could use a good DBA but to no avail. Oracle had been essentially eliminated from our enterprise. So, I did the next best thing: I helped Fred land an opportunity with Oracle Corporation where he has been happily employed ever since.

If you find that your career has turned into a cul-de-sac, my advice is head out the way you came in. Life is too short and workdays are too long to live in perpetual desperation. There's no honor in beating your head against the wall wishing it were different because the perfect fit may be waiting for you right around the corner. Go introduce yourself!

HOLE #8: DRESSED TO A TEE

A friend and I were recently discussing the lax dress code enforcement on most municipal golf courses nowadays. He could remember a time when he forgot his golf spikes and was forced to buy shoes in the pro shop before he could play. I relayed an amusing antidote about a co-worker who had worn jeans to an upscale private course. You won't get to read about it here, however, since that co-worker is now my wife and editor of these essays. That memoir is presently lying safely on the cutting room floor!

But what is the reasoning behind a dress code on the course? Presumably, by adhering to it, you're more likely to comply with golf's etiquette and rules. Might that also be the impetus behind corporate dress codes?

There may have been a dress code at my last office but it was not evident if there was. Many of our employees came to work in shorts and t-shirts. Call me "old school" but I would feel underdressed if I were wearing anything less than a pair of Dockers and a collared shirt, same as I would on any golf course. I just *thought* that was appropriate attire. When I consider it now, however, I realize it may have had more to do with how it made me *feel*.

A little over twenty years ago, I owned my own consulting firm and primarily worked out of my home. I spoke to my employees and customers over the phone and rarely met face to face with anyone. Nevertheless, I showered and dressed for work each morning as if I were going into the office instead of my basement. Who was that for if I was the only person present?

There is a relatively new school of thought called "enclothed cognition" that seeks to explain the effects of clothing on our cognitive processes. Through mental agility experiments, they have proven that a random group of people wearing lab coats actually made about half as many mistakes as people wearing just their street clothes! They further strengthened their theory when they gave identical lab coats to different volunteers but told one group that they were painter's smocks and the other, doctor's coats. The group wearing "doctor's coats" scored much better for the simple reason that we unconsciously attribute doctors with being smart.

"The clothes make the man" is attributed to Shakespeare and Mark Twain bolsters this argument by putting forth that "naked people have little or no influence on society." Now I don't know if wearing Dockers will make you smarter or a better golfer. But I highly recommend that by dressing **to** a "tee" rather than **in** one, you could improve your odds of success. Hey, it couldn't hurt!

HOLE #9: STOP AND SMELL THE PARS

A friend of mine recently got his third hole-in-one. I am not sure who was more excited, him or me. According to golf tradition, he is obligated to buy drinks for everyone on the course. God bless the Scots!

He asked if I've ever gotten a hole-in-one and I admitted that in 33 years, I had not. I joked that if I ever got one, I'd quit the game since I would have essentially grabbed the brass ring with no room for improvement. The fact of the matter was I was embarrassed that I hadn't. I had played a tremendous amount of golf and gotten my fair share of pars, birdies, and even an occasional eagle, but never scored an ace. I started thinking about how I felt about those multitudinal pars. Had I ever celebrated them? Not that I can recall. In fact, I had just gotten a par a few holes earlier but was disappointed because

I had missed the 5-foot putt for birdie. Frankly, you're supposed to get a par! That's what "par for the course" means!

And that is when it struck me. While pars are plentiful over the span of 33 years, they're not plentiful enough during a single round. If I could shoot 18 pars in a row, I would be a scratch golfer! And, I wouldn't have been in position to attempt that birdie putt unless I had hit the green in regulation. Therefore, a single par must also have some intrinsic value…as a means to an end, if nothing else. But I take them for granted and don't ever stop to celebrate them.

How often do we do the same thing at work? We achieve an incremental goal and, since it is not the ultimate finish line, we barely acknowledge the accomplishment. And yet, crossing that finish line is the culmination of crossing off a number of the incremental milestones. How do we measure success if our gauge is only calibrated to record the proverbial "hole-in-one"? Is our effectiveness simply reduced to "all or nothing"? When put that way, the absurdity is obvious but I must admit to being myopic a time or two in my career.

One of the things that have made me successful in business is my ability to reduce complex problems into progressively incremental improvements. My mantra is "to make tomorrow better than yesterday"; my goal is to keep the improvements self-contained so as to realize the benefits along the way. I once led a healthcare group that created an electronic data interchange with more than 100 insurance companies over the course of a single year. I tracked our progress on a common wall with pins stuck in a giant map of the United States. Each time a new insurance company was setup to bill electronically, our receivables from that company were reduced by about 90 days. It was a big deal and we were aptly rewarded for our efforts with an annual bonus.

But it wasn't sustainable. Our next goal was to double the previous year's number. Even though we brought on a new billing application to facilitate the process, the goal seemed too daunting and we slipped into a bit of a funk. By the end of January, we hadn't added a single electronic interchange! My team was burned out and I hadn't done anything to replenish their tank. So I ascribed a dollar value to each of our target companies according to the interest we would earn on their monthly AR. Each time we realized a gain of $1M to our bottom line, I held a celebration meeting where we recognized the contributors to our success. It didn't cost me a lot of time to prepare for and I don't think I ever spent more than $25 on each festivity, but the team thrived on the appreciation. In fact, it perpetuated it.

By the end of the year, we hadn't added the 200 companies that we had originally targeted; we added 320! We were so effective that there weren't any more companies to make electronic! And there was no post project hangover; the team was still energized to take on the next big thing. Our leadership was ecstatic as our efforts directly translated into an additional $20M per month to the bottom line. In their words, "You and your team aced it!" How appropriate that an "ace" is another name for a hole-in-one, one that we hit by stopping to "smell the pars" along the way.

HOLE #10: USING EVERYTHING IN YOUR BAG

Have you ever heard of the "One Club Challenge"? Many years ago, Seve Ballesteros, Nick Faldo, Lee Trevino, and Isao Aoki played the Old Course at St. Andrews with nothing more a 5-iron. While it made for interesting television to see these guys putt with an iron, I don't think it helped their scores too much. Whether you're hitting off the tee, out of the bunker, 150 yards out, or on the green, every club in your bag is designed to perform a specific job – unless you're still carrying a 1-iron because I have no idea what that thing is for! (Trevino once suggested holding it up in a lightning storm because "even God can't hit a 1-iron!") I have certain clubs that I use more than others (like my 4-iron for fairway shots >190 yards) but they're all there for a reason.

Now take a look at the team you're on at work and consider these two questions:

- Is everyone on the team being utilized for his or her strength?
- Is everyone on the team there for a reason…including you?

First question first – utilizing the person's strength: Have you ever had an employee who was in charge of something that was not in his wheelhouse? As I wrote about in "Grip It and Rip It", you can erroneously assign tasks that the individual is incapable of performing rather than considering his skills and interests. Or even worse, you can purposefully assign a task in order to address an employee's deficiencies; that is, you try to improve his poor performance by giving him more opportunities to increase his proficiency. I have yet to discover a justifiable reason to do this to someone. You wouldn't practice putting with your 5-iron when you have a perfectly good putter in your bag, would you? Of course not! It takes the same amount of effort to raise a skill from poor to mediocre as it does from good to great. Make a concerted effort to play to an individual's strengths.

If an individual's strength is not needed for a particular team we come to our second question: is everyone there for a reason? As I discussed in "The Pit of Despair", sometimes your team's charter shifts from database administration to software engineering. In that case, you need to help your expert DBA find a home on another team where he'll be successful. I promise he will thank you! Sometimes you may have an employee with no discernible strength, perhaps bouncing from one team to the next like a 1-iron. As unpalatable as it may seem, if you're the manager, you need to manage that individual out of the organization. While I can't promise it, he may actually thank you! Finally, you may find that you've simply worked yourself out of a job. For instance, your strength may be building high performing teams. As you do, you should also consider working on your succession plan. Once your high caliber team is built and showing its mettle, it is time to hand the reigns to your successor whose strength is managing high performing teams. While it may be comfortable to linger in the team that you just built, by taking my advice, handing it off, and building another, you'll thank me!

Each one of us is here for a reason. The trick is figuring out our "why" and then doing it as often as humanly possible.

HOLE #11: PRACTICE, PRACTICE, PRACTICE!

I've recently played with friends that golf maybe once or twice a year and it always amuses me when they get frustrated over an errant shot. I'm not sadistic, taking pleasure in other peoples' pain nor am I a proponent of the adage "misery loves company". What makes me laugh is when these "hackers" think that they can just show up and shoot well! The reason behind their delusions of grandeur is that these guys are athletic and therefore proficient at most sports that they have attempted: baseball, football, and soccer. Despite the fact that the ball is just laying still on the ground before you hit it, golf is probably the hardest sport you will ever attempt to play. Just think about all of the complexities! You're hitting a 1.68" ball with a 4' stick into a 4.25" hole that is .28

miles away from where you started! If that isn't enough to convince you, you have to put it in the hole with 5 hits or less (by the way, a swing and a miss still counts as 1)!

While my fellow hackers show up to the course with their natural athleticism and expecting to do well, Lee Trevino said, "There is no such thing as a natural touch. Touch is something you create by hitting millions of golf balls." Look at Tiger Woods who possibly has the most natural swing ever. When asked by a fan how much he practices, he answered between seven and eight hours a day. So the two practice swings that my biannual golfing buddies take on the first tee aren't enough to guarantee par?

Say what you will about Tiger's quality of game lately, he's won 14 major championships and still spends a third of the day practicing. You may argue that he practices so much because he's a professional and golfing is his job. Okay, fair point. Then why do we think that we can show up to our jobs without practicing? I've been in management for over twenty years now (about the same amount of time that Tiger has been a pro) and I constantly find myself needing to hone my skills. I just graduated last month from Leadership Acceleration Program[v] (LEAP) and over the course of the year, made a startling new discovery! To this point, my career had been focused on "what" and "how"; that is, what do we need to do and how are we going to get there. A very tactical approach and I was good at it. As I mentioned in my introduction, I thoroughly enjoy finding solutions to business problems. But then I realized that I had overlooked a very important factor, namely "why". Why did I get out of bed each morning? (Aside from the fact that I get to eat bacon everyday for breakfast – which is the greatest meat ever invented and God's way of showing us that He loves us!) Why did my organization exist? And finally, why was I working in that particular organization? I quickly realized that I didn't have a good answer and probably needed to be doing something else. It was no longer enough that I was good at what I was doing; I needed to love it. But I wouldn't have come to this game-changing conclusion unless I had taken the time to "practice" and discover a missing aspect of my "game". My "why" is simply to **help unlock human potential by facilitating their journey from good to great.** Have you ever coached someone and witnessed him "getting it"? I live for that moment!

So whether you're an individual contributor developing a skill or a leader inspiring others to follow, you need to make time to practice. Sometimes that can simply mean reading a book on a particular subject while other times it requires more reflection on recent successes and determining a way to expand them. Learning is defined as the acquisition of skills or knowledge and one way to acquire them is through practice!

GOLF SWING

THE X-FACTOR

HOLE #12: THE "X-FACTOR"

I've often wondered why there is so much disparity in my golf scores. On Monday I can shoot an 81 and Tuesday, a 99! I am the same player with the same clubs on the very same golf course but producing a very different outcome from one day to the next.

As I've mentioned in previous essays, golf is a very complex sport and difficult to master. I suppose that's one of the attractions – if it were easy, it would be boring. Your four basic shots (drive, fairway, chip, and putt) all have to work harmoniously in order to score well. There is a saying that I have proven true: "Drive for show and putt for dough." I've started a hole really well off the tee only to three-putt and end up taking a double bogey.

But none of that accounts for the severe variation in my score. My proficiency should not be so fluid but some days it just is. Why?

- It could be something as simple as using a different golf ball. I lived on a course for 7 years and, as a result, have collected more assorted balls in my yard than I will ever use. Some balls are designed to go straighter while others go further. Depending on the ball I choose that day, I may get a different result.

- I have a very bad back that flares up from time to time and can restrict my mobility. When it is particularly out, I can actually feel myself pulling everything to the left because of it.

- The weather can also play a huge part in the distance your ball travels. When the ball and club are colder, the transfer of energy is not as efficient, so the ball speed will be less. In addition, cold air is denser than warm air, causing more resistance and drag. Conversely, humidity reduces density because water vapor is lighter than dry air; therefore, your ball will fly further in higher humidity.

These variables are all "X-Factors" because they are all outside of my control. And I've not only experienced them in golf, they also pop up in business! Have you ever successfully done a job ten times in a row but the eleventh time goes horribly wrong? What was your unaccounted for X-Factor?

- A downturn in the economy

- A leadership breakdown at the top
- A failure to communicate a clear, concise value proposition to your team

This last one involving communication caught me quite by surprise early on in my career. I had been making a living by rescuing stalled projects and pushing them across the finish line. The tricky part of operating in that niche is that you're always starting behind the eight ball so there isn't much room for error.

My Myers Briggs personality registers as an ENTJ[vi], which is described as the Marshall or Commander. I had successfully used my intrinsically direct method of communication for years but this one particular team that I managed seemed impervious. I couldn't understand it. I was practicing the Golden Rule and treating them exactly the way I would like to be treated.

And that's when the X-Factor hit me! What if this group didn't like being treated like me? ENTJs make up such a small portion of the population (which is not an accident because we'd kill each other if there were more of us). So I quickly gave the assessment to each member of the team and found that most were INTJs[vii], described as the Architect or Mastermind. Even though we were ¾ the same, there was a major difference. INTJs like to consider all of the possible permutations before committing to a goal; whereas, I was more of a Larry the Cable Guy – "Git 'r done!"

I realized that I was already waiting at the bottom

line for the rest of my team to finish evaluating their options, thereby leaving both sides frustrated. I simply needed to slow down and spend more time communicating our value proposition…and it worked like a charm! It worked so well that I dubbed my newfound skill, "The Platinum Rule: Treating others the way they like to be treated." (Turns out that a really smart guy named Tony Alessandra[viii] had already published my discovery with the exact same name back in 1996.)

Nevertheless, I had removed an X-Factor by shifting it to within my sphere of control. As a result, I became a much better leader by tailoring my communications according to the needs of the individuals receiving them.

HOLE #13: NEVER GIVE UP! NEVER SURRENDER!

I was having an unusually bad day at golf. On one hole in particular I was already 2 over par with a 10-foot putt in front of me. My golfing buddy asked if I surrender. In my best Winston Churchill impersonation I replied, "Never give up! Never surrender!" Turns out I was misremembering the Prime Minister's famous speech and was actually reciting Tim Allen's lines from Galaxy Quest (which was an awesome movie, by the way). Despite my historical faux pas, my sentiment remains. If we were holding up a group behind us, etiquette would dictate picking up my ball at that point. But we weren't and so there was no compelling reason to quit. Nevertheless, many of us would in that situation. In fact, that same golf buddy had suddenly walked off the course last year mid-round because he was playing so poorly that day.

I thought about that episode again last night and wondered if there was an advantage to not surrendering or if my hard, Irish head would simply not let me quit. I came up with a few clichés:

- Practice makes perfect (though "perfect" doesn't ever happen in golf!)
- Whatever doesn't kill you makes you stronger
- Giving up is the only sure way to fail
- Failure is not the opposite of success, it's part of success

That last one always reminds me of Thomas Edison. The story goes that "Thomas Edison failed more than 1,000 times when trying to create the light bulb". (Sometimes it is told as 5,000 or 10,000 times, depending on the version.) When asked about it, Edison allegedly said, "I have not failed 1,000 times. I have successfully discovered 1,000 ways to NOT make a light bulb."

Why do we often think there is nothing valuable in our failure? I recently wrote a book called "Sixteen Things I Know", subtitled "Usually by doing it wrong the first time." Most of what I've truly learned has included mistakes along the way. In fact, many of these essays begin with my misstep or misconception. As a kid I had a really hard job selling newspaper subscriptions door to door. I was terrible at it because I was so afraid of rejection that I would never ask for the sale. But I hung in there and eventually learned not to take "no" so personally and become their number one salesman.

Are there times in business when we should just give up? Perhaps, though I can't think of any at the moment. A better course of action would be figuring out what isn't going well and adjust accordingly. For example:

- If you love what you're doing but not the people you're doing it with, find somewhere else to pursue your passion. The culture where you are is simply not a good fit for you.
- If you hate every moment of what you're doing, do something else! Life is too short to not do what you love (or at least like).
- If you've got more money going out than you have coming in, you either need to get a higher paying job or adopt a more modest standard of living.

At this point, I'm feeling a bit like Captain Obvious but my point is simply this: Don't give up just because what you're doing seems hard or fruitless. You may miss an opportunity for a life lesson. That 10-foot putt I mentioned earlier...I made it and it gave me a lot more confidence on the next green. Having more doors slammed in my face than newspaper subscriptions sold accounted for eventual self-assurance and emotional stability. Keep on keeping on.

HOLE #14: THINKING VERSUS LISTENING

Depending on the time we start and the amount of daylight remaining, my foursome will sometimes play the same course twice in one day. It always amazes me that the second time through, I'll not only remember where I hit the previous round's tee shots but also other guys' shots as well. And it is not just me, they will recall them, too. I have a hard time remembering a person's name when introduced and yet I can recall the flight of a ball hit 4 hours ago? How can this be?

Simple. In golf, your foursome takes the tee and the three players not hitting all stand behind the one who is. Etiquette dictates that you not speak or move around at this point. Our undivided attention is solely concentrated on helping the player teeing off to subsequently locate his ball. Conversely, when I meet someone at a party, I'm distracted. I'm processing their physical appearance (unconsciously judging them) while I'm thinking of something clever to say. During this information overload, their name is spoken and typically goes in one ear and out the other. It's not my memory that is failing me; it is my failure to pay attention.

Have you ever been in a meeting where you were so distracted by crafting your point in your head that you missed what others were saying? I noticed this was happening a lot in my homeroom meetings. When I first started managing my team, I was amazed to find that many of my employees had never actually spoken to one another. In order to remedy this, I scheduled 12-minute daily, stand-up meetings in my office and each would take a minute or two to discuss their "hot topic du jour". While it managed to get all my engineers speaking aloud, I noticed a lot of redundancy and overlap in each one's subject matter.

I began watching the team members that were not speaking and found they were also not listening. In some cases, I noticed their lips silently moving and quickly surmised that they were rehearsing their topic while waiting for their turn to speak. I tested my theory by surreptitiously asking an engineer what he thought about the update that was given right before him. Invariably, he would look at me like a dog looks at a ceiling fan! He had no idea what was said; he wasn't listening.

Without announcement or fanfare, I made two minor adjustments that yielded the results that I desired. I called on individuals to give their update based on the order in which they had arrived for the meeting, thereby making it appear random. Secondly, I would periodically ask the speaker to draw from experience and offer his perspective on the previous engineer's update. The difference was like night and day. The more they interacted, the more they enjoyed interacting. When someone from another part of the company was visiting our office, our team would invite that person to our homeroom and encourage them to speak. Our group of introverts became a high performing team, collaborating on issues and facilitating their own "homeroom-type" venues.

Most of the team has gone on to the next step in their career, seeding other teams and making them great. Our success was lauded by leadership and became a template for others to follow. The only thing they needed to unlock their true potential was simply to listen to one another.

HOLE #15: I CANNOT TELL A LIE

Isn't it ironic that the only professional sport where you keep your own score is replete with the word "lie"? In the game of golf, the word "lie" can refer to:

- How your ball is sitting on the grass? A good lie is when it's sitting on the fairway, a bad lie is when it's buried in the rough, and an uneven lie is when it's on the slope of a hill.

- If you're lying 4, that means that it has taken you 4 strokes to advance your ball to this point.

- And my favorite lie: "Put me down for a par."

I used to sit out in my backyard, which was just off the left side of the 18th green, and listen to that last lie all day long. I could hear the players tee off on this short par 4, slicing the ball out of bounds and into the houses on the right. According to the "stroke and distance rule", that meant they had to take a penalty and were lying 3 by the time they hit safely off the tee. If you added a chip onto the green and 2 putts, by my calculations that would total 6 strokes (or a double bogey). But I wish I had a nickel for every time I heard someone say instead, "Put me down for a par." It used to make me snicker every time.

I often wondered, "What does that guy get out of lying on his own scorecard?" Perhaps he was not taking ownership specifically of his mistakes nor for his game in general. And if you lie when nothing is on the line (as he did in a friendly game of golf), what will you do when you face adversity at work? When I was a child, I used to be terrified of being wrong and found it damn near impossible to admit it when I was. I'd make up all kinds of reasons and excuses as to why I was "technically correct" if viewed from a particular point of view. I guess I eventually got over it by observing that the overwhelming number of mistakes I made did not lead to my extermination. As I recently wrote about in "Never Give Up! Never Surrender!", I now find a lot of value in my failures. In fact when I am interviewing someone, I am particularly interested in the "Tell me about a time you failed" question. I'm looking for self-awareness, growth, and above all, honesty.

I know what you're thinking, "But there's a guy at work that only lies when his lips are moving and gets nothing but accolades and promotions! What about him?" Am I close? Yes, I know *that guy*, too. In fact, I once had a candid conversation with him and was absolutely stunned by something he divulged. He was aware of his lack of honesty and carried it around with him like a millstone, in constant fear of being exposed as a fraud. When I asked him why he didn't just admit his mistakes when he made them, he revealed he was afraid that by doing so, people might not like him. He was so terrified of what others thought that he created a whole different persona and was now living a lie. He appeared to be successful and quickly rising up the corporate ladder though I couldn't help but pity him for the cost with which he was now burdened. He could be completely undone at any moment.

When I was in high school, my father told me that the only thing I truly owned was my word and to not give it away frivolously. He couldn't have been more right. There was a time later in life when I was completely wiped out and the only thing I had left was my word. I used it to rebuild and within a few short years, had restored all the things that were taken from me. Being authentic and transparent is not only profitable, it is freeing. Just do your best and own the results. If you make a mistake, learn from it, don't lie about it. Who knows? It may make a great story the next time you're interviewing!

HOLE #16: REAL DIVERSITY

The rainy season has started again in the Great Northwest and some of the putting greens have large, persistent puddles on them. As a result, the groundskeepers are not cutting the greens quite as often and in some cases, not at all. Such was the case with hole #11. My foursome had all reached the green in regulation and each of us was in a position to 2-putt for par. But this green more closely resembled a shag carpet than a putting surface. The first guy in my group putted the ball as if we were still on the previous green and it rolled halfway to the hole before stopping. The second guy was obviously not a history major because he putted with exactly the same result. The third, not willing to conform to the demonstrated insanity of the first two, putted his ball so hard that it left the green entirely. My turn. I took a pitching wedge out of my bag and chipped the ball right next to the hole. The third guy exclaimed that he had never seen anyone use a wedge on the green! I assured him that while it may be a bit unorthodox, it is still a legal shot and a better alternative considering the conditions.

My friends are all more experienced golfers than I am. Yet, they had fallen prey to conventional wisdom (you drive with a driver and putt with a putter) despite the circumstances warranting a different response. And that is the precise reason that experts can sometimes suffer from myopia.

Consider the poor fellow that went to a renowned ENT to cure his persistent earache. The doctor prescribed the correct medicine and wrote instructions for his physician's assistant to administer 3 drops in the right ear. In his haste, he abbreviated one crucial word: "Put 3 drops in R ear." The PA, not wanting to question the expert doctor, put the drops in the patient's hindquarters. More surprisingly, the patient allowed her to do this because he thought that they were the medical experts! While the patient suffered no lasting side effects, he left the doctor's office with a little less dignity and an earache.

I recently applied for a senior producer position with a video game company. It seemed like the perfect combination of project management and creative development for my next vocational challenge. The hiring manager wrote back to me, "It's a senior role, so we're looking for prior experience. It's difficult to break in fresh from outside the industry, as opposed to coming up through the ranks."

Is he correct? I don't know. I've never worked in the gaming industry before. But I do know that almost every job application includes a diversity page that asks about my race and gender. Presumably, this helps employers draw from an array of different life experiences that will contribute to the success of both the employee and the company.

When I made the move from DaVita to T-Mobile, I was surrounded by brilliant people that had spent their entire career in telecommunications. Healthcare has a challenging lexicon but this new industry embeds acronyms inside of other acronyms. It took me weeks to decipher that my employees were in fact speaking English! At the beginning of my tenure, I asked a lot of questions and was amazed at one recurring response: "Because we've always done it that way." One of the contributions that I offered to our success was a "diverse perspective" to the problems that we faced. I would suggest a "pitching wedge" when they considered a "putter" as the only viable solution.

In his book <u>A Whole New Mind</u>[ix], Daniel Pink writes, "While detailed knowledge of a single area once guaranteed success, today the top rewards go to those who can operate with equal aplomb in starkly different realms." If we want to achieve real diversity in the workplace, we need to begin by forming teams from a variety of experiences.

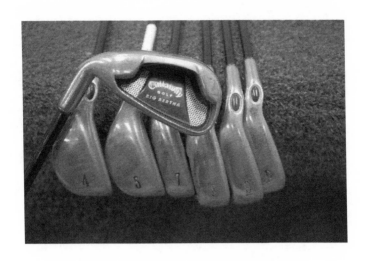

HOLE #17: STRETCH

I have been playing golf with a guy that, in the 8 months that I've known him, has purchased two brand new sets of clubs. Each time he swears that his game magically improves and he has been encouraging me to trade in my 15 year old Callaways. But during that same time, my score has varied from 71 to 101 so I know it's not the club, rather it's the consistency of the guy swinging it. My golf buddy's quest for success through the latest technology alone will prove to be utterly self-defeating.

Have you ever run across that same sentiment at work? "The only thing holding us back is the acquisition of this system or that one." Having worked in tech my entire life, of course I would almost always advocate for better systems. But is that the only thing that is holding you back? Have you completely exhausted every other possible improvement? My wife likes to say that when you point your finger, there are always four fingers pointing back at you. (To which I always *point* out that the thumb is technically running parallel to the index finger thereby leaving only three fingers pointing back at me. At which *point* I get "the sigh and the look" from her!) Anyway, the *point* is that while we pine for solutions outside the sphere of our control, there are often times incremental improvements that we could be making inside of that sphere.

When I started my last job, there was an operational dashboard that graphically showed the last two weeks of our service's performance. Often a spike in the graph (usually downward) would garner our leadership's attention and necessitate an explanation from one of our engineers. More often than not, "the pointy thing" was actually within normal parameters and was simply exaggerated by the minute scale on the y-axis. I asked my group why they hadn't modified the dashboard to appropriately reflect "normal behavior"? They replied it was scheduled to be replaced by a more comprehensive, sophisticated system.

"When will we get this new system?" I asked.

"In about a year or two," they replied.

"In the meantime, we'll keep raising false alarms that require an engineer to investigate?"

No one answered my rhetorical question but the look on their faces clearly indicated that they hadn't considered any other alternatives. I'll spare you the nerdy math details but by merely using median and first standard deviation, we were able to plot what "good" looked like on the dashboard. We reduced the number of calls from our Senior Vice President by a factor of 20! All of that "new, free time" was invested back into making our metrics more predictive of a failure rather than reporting when they had already occurred. We shifted our focus from fixing problems to avoiding them in the first place and finally achieved the elusive five 9's of availability. (To my non-operations friends, that's less than 5 1/4 minutes of downtime per year!)

We were so successful that the aforementioned "new system" was abandoned and the entire organization adopted our process. Even our product vendor, responsible for monitoring service uptime, asked permission to use our metrics. Probably the most surprising aspect is that we were able to accomplish all of this with the tools and knowledge we already had on-hand. Could we have benefited from garnering a new system? Maybe. Or it might have just introduced new problems. Either way, we most certainly benefited by stretching the resources we already had.

HOLE #18: GREAT EXPECTATIONS

Don't worry! Despite the title of my final chapter, I have no intention of recapping Charles Dickens' penultimate novel. Instead, I seek to understand why my best golf scores come when no witnesses are there to see it. Several weeks ago I played the course alone because none of the guys were available. I did exceedingly well! In fact, I shot a 71 – the best score I've ever gotten. I just couldn't miss. I told my golf buddies all about the previous day and then proceeded to shoot a 93! Where did that guy go who shot so well the day before? Skeptics would assume that I was cheating but I assure you I did not. I was perplexed.

Then I read about a horse named Hans who lived around the end of the nineteenth century. His owner, William, was a German mathematician and had ostensibly taught Hans how to do math problems. When William wrote two numbers on the blackboard and asked to sum them, Hans would stomp out the correct answer with his hoof. Everyone naturally assumed it was a trick so in 1904, a commission came together to investigate. Surprisingly, they found that Hans could perform just about as well with William as without him. They concluded that the horse was legit and could really do math with his hoof. They started calling him Clever Hans.

It was another three years before biologist and psychologist, Oskar Pfungst, figured out what was really going on. Hans was truly clever but not in the sense that the commission deemed him. Oskar found that when the person asking the question didn't know the answer, Hans didn't either. He demonstrated that the horse was not actually solving the problem; he was reacting to subtle cues. The tension in the questioner's posture and facial expression changed when Hans made the final and correct tap. Thus, the horse knew when to stop tapping his hoof.

As a brand new supervisor, I was a huge proponent of "you get what you inspect". That meant that my team was paid to do the work and I was paid to ensure that it got done. I was very effective and our team got more stuff done than any other. However, the weeks that I'd go on vacation, it seemed like the rest of my team did too! Nothing got done because I wasn't there inspecting them. Later in my career, I made one minor tweak that made all of the difference: "You get what you expect."

I had started at T-Mobile a few weeks after they announced the acquisition by AT&T. To say that morale was low would be an understatement. People were jumping ship left and right and those that stayed had checked out mentally. I took my team into a conference room and told them that, regardless of what might happen in the future, we were being paid to do a job today. I expected them to not only do their job but to become the "greatest engineering team that T-Mobile has ever seen." I explained that I had already been through two M&As and the best way you keep your job is by making yourself invaluable. And the means we would use to measure our success was by other groups starting to copy what we were doing. This accomplished two things: my team had an incentive to work hard and also to share everything they knew with their coworkers.

The government ended up quashing the AT&T deal and we all kept our jobs. But by then, we had become the greatest engineering team that T-Mobile had ever seen! The advances we made in operational metrics, uptime, business intelligence, and training became standards for the entire organization. I have never seen a better group of engineers come together more effectively in the face of adversity. You see, my golf game improved because I expected to do well and wasn't reacting to the guys in my foursome. William expected his horse to do math and Hans reacted to him. And I expected my team to do well and they all reacted to and collaborated with one another. For better or worse, you get what you expect.

HOLE #19: CONCLUSION

The 19th hole is a euphemism for the place where golfers go afterwards to reflect on their game, also known as the bar. Hopefully someone shot a hole-in-one that day, in which case, they are buying the first round! At this point, I invite you to get up and pour yourself a tall one as we review together the lessons learned in this book. Seriously, go get yourself a drink; I've got mine! I'll wait.....

Back so soon? Terrific. Cheers! Okay, now where were we? Ah, yes, lessons I have learned from the game of golf summary:

1. **A Drive and a Putt:** Don't get too caught up in quantifying my failures, especially when I have negatively affected my customers. It's not fair that my big and small outages have the same weight just like it's not fair that a drive and a putt both count as 1 stroke. Get over it.

Life is not fair. I need to learn from my mistakes and make sure I don't make a habit out of the same ones!

2. **Forest Through the Trees:** When I do find myself in the midst of a mistake, stop making it worse by trying to plow through it! When my project has gotten lost in the woods, I need to take the most direct route out, which sometimes is backwards. It won't feel good going sideways instead of forward but it feels a lot better than a ricochet to the head! Discretion is the better part of valor.

3. **The Competition:** We have met the competition and he is us! I don't really need to compete with anyone on the team besides myself. My coworker is not my opponent; in fact, I make the team stronger by sharing solutions to problems that I've discovered along the way. Knowledge is power but only if it is shared.

4. **Squirrel!:** In a world where Attention Deficit is ubiquitous, I need to remember to keep my eye on the ball. Allowing distractions to break my train of thought causes disruptions in "my flow". Best case, it will take me twenty minutes to refocus on the task at hand. Worst case, too many squirrels can steer my entire project off course.

5. **One Bite at a Time:** Incrementalism is the key to successful change. Trying to modify too many things simultaneously often leads to a jumbled mess. Now I simply try to make tomorrow look better than yesterday.

6. **Grip It and Rip It:** Going from poor to

mediocre takes as much effort as going from good to great. I need to concentrate on doing more of what I'm good at and find others to fill in my deficiencies. When I'm building a team, don't just take into account someone's aptitude, also consider their passions and desire.

7. **The Pit of Despair:** If I ever find myself in the proverbial Pit of Despair, it may be time to make a change. While I control my desire and ability, my boss dictates the opportunity and no amount of wishing the contrary will make it otherwise. Life is too short to accept the life you have than to find the one you love.

8. **Dressed to a Tee:** Sometimes something as simple as my clothes will not only dictate how I feel about myself but also has a direct correlation on how I perform. It is important to set myself up for success by factoring in even the small contributors.

9. **Stop and Smell the Pars:** And while I am on that long road to success, it is critical to acknowledge the gains along the way. Very few holes are played with just one swing and very few projects are completed in one day. I need to take time to celebrate along the way.

10. **Using Everything in Your Bag:** We all have a purpose and it is important to identify mine and ensure that I am living up to my potential. Just because I can successfully do a job doesn't mean that I should continue doing it at the expense of my true talent. You can putt with a five-iron but why would you want to?

11. **Practice, Practice, Practice!:** Why I do what

I do is just as important, if not more so, than what. Once I have identified my "why" and unique set of skills for accomplishing it, I shouldn't rest on my laurels. I need to continue to practice my craft and find better ways of doing something. If I'm not learning, I'm not growing. And if I'm not growing, I'm dying.

12. **The "X-Factor":** I need to always consider that there may be new variables affecting my success. What worked with one team may not transfer to the next and it is important to determine if these factors are inside my sphere of control. If so, I need to make the appropriate accommodations to overcome.

13. **Never Give Up! Never Surrender!:** Growth comes through the struggle and it is important to remember not to surrender when things seem hopeless. I have learned a great deal from my failures and I need to consider them part of my success. While I may need to shift my focus from time to time, I haven't truly failed until I have given up completely.

14. **Thinking versus Listening:** I should always listen to understand rather than to respond. When I am thinking about what I'm going to say, I may be missing a salient point. Listening to one another leads to collaboration which unlocks our fullest potential.

15. **I Cannot Tell a Lie:** My word is the only thing I truly own and should not be given lightly. Truth is the only basis for a relationship and I should never fear the consequences of being authentic. If I make a

mistake, I should admit it and move on. And if someone (including myself) can learn something from it, bonus!

16. **Real Diversity:** When I build my teams, I need to not only consider the obvious diversity dynamics but also the diversity of thought. It may be more comfortable to form a group of likeminded individuals but that would make us one dimensional. True rewards come from starkly different realms.

17. **Stretch:** When I'm looking for a solution, I need to consider that I may already have it in my toolbox. Getting the next shiny new thing seems exciting but it could also bring a whole new set of challenges. It may not be the club that needs replacing but an incremental tweak to my swing.

18. **Great Expectations:** There is something almost magical about getting what you expect. If I think it will probably go wrong, I am probably right. The way to get the most out of life is to expect great things (from myself and others) and let the laws of gravity do the rest.

19. **Conclusion:** If I ever do get a hole-in-one, I'll never tell! Buying drinks for the entire golf course can get expensive! I'll just rest in the success and privately bask in the glory!

That's it! Folksy business wisdom...hopefully nothing earth shattering or too convoluted. I hope that I have inspired you to blend your work and life passions to gain balance. As I alluded to in the introduction, my intent for you was two-fold: foremost, to entertain and secondarily, to give you an alternative solution to a problem you may be facing. If I have accomplished either, I count it as gain. If I accomplished both, a miracle! Thank you for reading!

ABOUT THE AUTHOR

Originally hailing from Philadelphia, Tom (only his best friend and loving wife, Kristi, calls him "Thomas") now makes his home in the Greater Seattle Area. Entrepreneur, author, business leader, lecturer, and humorist, Tom spends what little time remains out on the golf course with his buddies: Ken, Mike, Tom (different guy, same name), Frank, Devin, Erik, and even Kevin.

Tom has been working in technology since 1985 (yes, there were computers back then!) and holds two patents on his medical credentialing software. He has become proficient in spotting the things that divide our companies and has developed a comprehensive way of uniting them around a common goal. His surgical approach combined with his unique sense of humor has delivered much needed cross-functional synergies that he openly shares with companies and professional organizations.

Thomas J. McSweeney Jr.

i https://www.linkedin.com/in/mcsweeneytom/

ii http://www.lakewildernessgc.com/-course

iii http://www.clubatsnoqualmieridge.com/golf/course

iv https://www.youtube.com/watch?v=1dSrkoGR90w

v http://www.leadership-acceleration.com/

vi https://www.16personalities.com/entj-personality

vii https://www.16personalities.com/intj-personality

viii https://www.linkedin.com/in/tonyalessandra/

ix https://en.wikipedia.org/wiki/A_Whole_New_Mind